Hank the Hiking Hound

And

Lessons From The Trail

Hank the Hiking Hound

And

Lessons From The Trail

Mitch Emmons

Xulon Press

Dedication...

With much love to our grands - Tyler, Trent, Anne, and Jackson. May you each know the Lord and have blessed and fulfilling lives.

Xulon Press
2301 Lucien Way #415
Maitland, FL 32751
407.339.4217
www.xulonpress.com

© 2023 by Mitch Emmons

All rights reserved solely by the author. The author guarantees all contents are original and do not infringe upon the legal rights of any other person or work. No part of this book may be reproduced in any form without the permission of the author.

Due to the changing nature of the Internet, if there are any web addresses, links, or URLs included in this manuscript, these may have been altered and may no longer be accessible. The views and opinions shared in this book belong solely to the author and do not necessarily reflect those of the publisher. The publisher therefore disclaims responsibility for the views or opinions expressed within the work.

Unless otherwise indicated, Scripture quotations taken from the Holy Bible, New International Version (NIV). Copyright © 1973, 1978, 1984, 2011 by Biblica, Inc.™. Used by permission. All rights reserved.

Paperback ISBN-13: 978-1-66287-741-4
Hard Cover ISBN-13: 978-1-66287-742-1
Ebook ISBN-13: 978-1-66287-743-8

About the Cover: *Hank atop Mount Cheaha at Sunset* — Rising to a height of 2,413 feet, Mount Cheaha is the highest land point in the State of Alabama. This photograph was awarded Honorable Mention in the Cheaha State Park's 2022 photography contest. To me, however, Hank takes the grand prize!

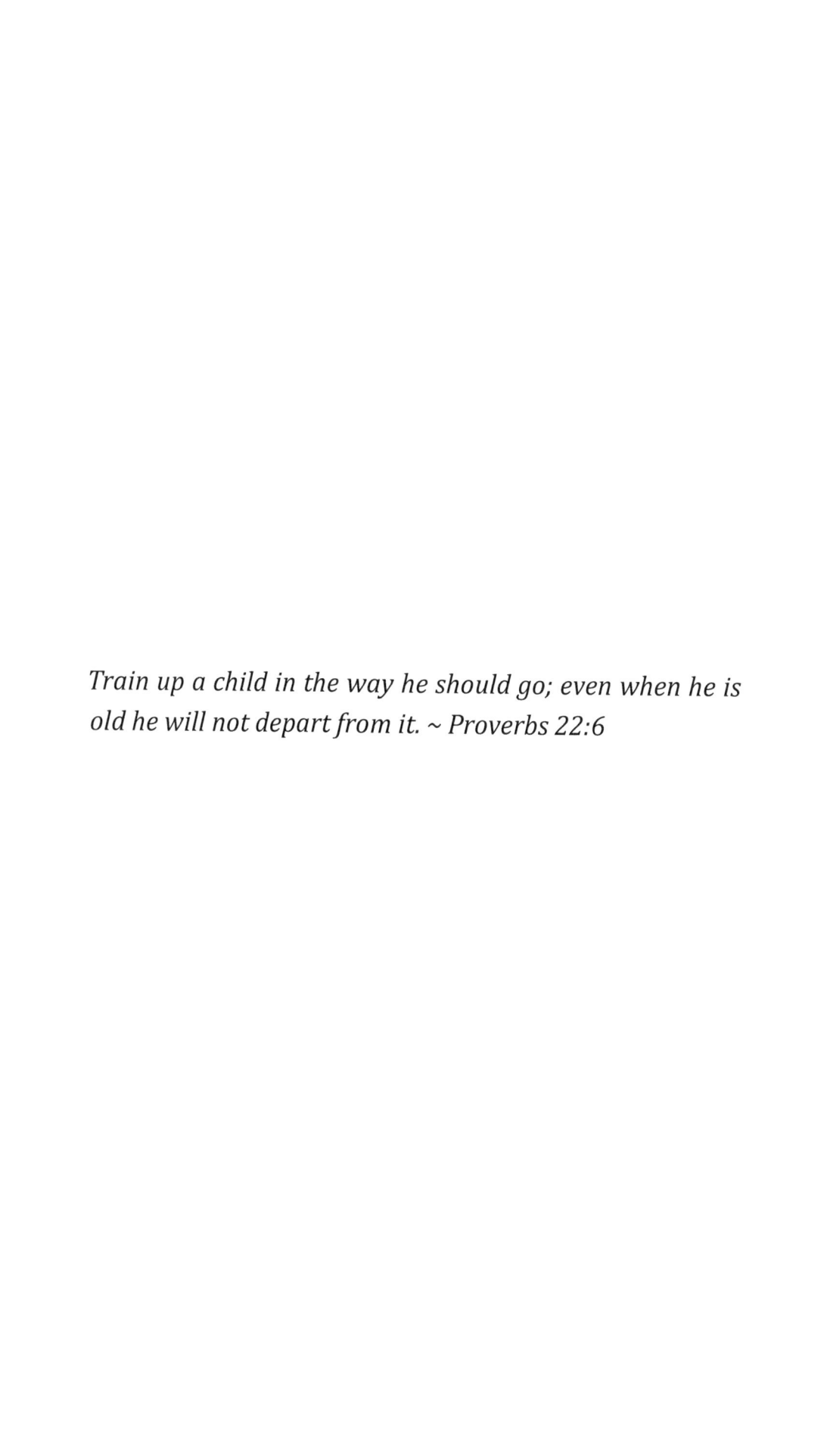

Train up a child in the way he should go; even when he is old he will not depart from it. ~ Proverbs 22:6

Contents

Dedication iv

Prologue viii

1. The Water is Good 1

2. It's Cold and Dark. 4

3. Keep Good Company 7

4. Leadership. 10

5. Trust Him 13

6. Follow the Blaze. 17

7. Carry Your Weight 19

8. Feed the Spirit 22

9. Rest is Best 25

10. Joy is Strength 28

11. Peace, Be Still 31

12. Finish Well 35

Dedication... ~ vii

Prologue

I have been a journalist and photographer all of my working life. I've written countless news articles and stories for newspapers, magazines, and various types of publications. I have received awards for my writing and photography; however, I have never written a book.

I have friends who have, and I have given thought to the idea, but I talk myself out of it just as quickly, reasoning that I have nothing to write that is worthy of more than a news article-type (e.g., short) treatment. What do I have to say that requires book-length treatment and could possibly hold the interest of a reader for that length of time?

I've considered myself to be a Christian for many years. I was baptized in the church at the ripe age of sixteen. I went to Sunday school, to church, and socialized with the other church youth, but I was never consistent about reading the Bible and studying God's Word. I never really understood the fullness obtainable by walking daily with the Lord in Scripture. And let me tell you, I strayed.

Nevertheless, I went on to have a regular kind of life with a family and a career. Everything was going along like it should, right?

That changed a few years ago as I was reaching the time of my long-anticipated retirement. I lost my wife, Gloria, of thirty-six years to cancer. It was a battle that she fought bravely to the end, which came after almost six months in a hospital intensive care unit.

I am only now realizing how much God has used and continues to use that tragedy to help me grow in my relationship with Him. During that hospital time, I was forever changed. I was changed by the experience itself, by the people I encountered during that time and since, and by the sharing of that battle with my wife who, through it all, maintained a steadfast faith in the Lord, Jesus Christ our Savior. Her struggles and enduring strength and bravery began to show me where I had fallen terribly short in my own relationship with God.

She went to be with the Lord, but not before leaving me with specific instructions about how to carry on in her absence and how to be assured that I would be okay for the rest of my journey on Earth without her.

This was a blessing and a gift that I only now am fully appreciating.

Time passed. Much of it very difficult. I dealt with tremendous grief and anger and suffered a period of near insanity. Somewhere during that struggle, I met Suz, the beautiful lady who also became my wife. Suz picked up where Gloria left off, pointing me down a path of God's will and helping me to stay on it.

And then came Hank.

I have enjoyed an avid interest in hiking and backpacking over the years since entering retirement. I've hiked with small groups of friends and I've hiked with Suz, but much of the time, I've hiked alone.

Hank came to us with the addition of a new grandchild and a need to find a new home for this large, gentle giant of a dog. We don't know much about Hank's pedigree since he was a rescue, but we believe that he is a Plott Hound/Labrador Retriever mix, about seven or eight years old when we met him. What we do know is that Hank is a great dog who has become my constant companion on the trail.

In the short time that he has been with us, Hank has joined me on numerous hikes and backpacking trips for hundreds of miles on trails throughout my home state of Alabama as well as in Georgia, Tennessee, the Carolinas, and Virginia, and on such well-known trails as the Pinhoti, the Appalachian Trail, through the Cheaha and Sipsey Wilderness Areas of the Talladega and Bankhead National Forests, respectively, and many others. Moreover, in 2022, Hank became the first dog on record to complete the sixty-mile set of loop trails that comprise the "Alabama Triple Crown of Backpacking."

Hank is a natural on the trail, and since he makes friends wherever he goes, he is becoming quite the "rock star." So, when I mentioned again the idea of perhaps writing a book, Suz quickly suggested that it could be a book for young readers about Hank and his hiking adventures.

So, here it is - a compilation of short adventure stories starring Hank the hiking hound and featuring some of the photographs I have taken along the trail. My hope through this effort is to provide the young reader with a bit of entertainment while helping to instill a love of animals, an appreciation for nature and the outdoors, empathy about situations that can be hard ones to navigate, and the value of friendship, loyalty, leadership, and service.

Prologue ~ ix

Most of all, I hope to use this as a way to share God's Word in an encouraging way and to encourage those who read this to spend more time studying Scripture. Hiking in God's creation has brought me closer to Him. I am no longer young, but I am studying God's Word now in earnest. I am still learning and growing in my relationship with Him. I always will be, but Hank and others are helping to teach me.

1

The Water is Good

It was Hank's first time on a real hiking trail. Hank was a town dog. He had been taken on walks before, but always on a leash and always along a city street or sidewalk.

This was a new kind of experience. There was no street or sidewalk, only a dirt path. There were trees, big rocks, and hills all around. There was grass, flowers, and all manner of living creatures and smells to grab Hank's attention. This was different, indeed. To Hank, this was exciting!

Devil's Den Falls along the Chinabee Silent Trail, Mount Cheaha State Park

Hank loved to walk, and out there, he could walk and walk... and he did. He got thoroughly caught up in and happy about his walking and with all of the distractions that abounded. Eventually, he grew tired and thirsty, but where was his water bowl? Someone had always made sure that his water bowl was full and that he had fresh water to drink.

Hank looked around and saw no water bowl, but he did see a fast running stream and the stream looked cool and inviting. So, he bounded over and lapped up a taste. It must have been very refreshing as he drank more. After a bit, Hank was ready to walk some more.

There is an idiom — a cultural saying — among people in the hiking and backpacking community: "The trail will provide." In the situation of providing a water source for Hank, that is true in the literal sense. Hank learned an important lesson on his first ever hike. He learned how to find good water along the trail and that when a drink is made available, he should take that drink to sustain him for the rest of his journey.

Water sources found along the trail are a creation of God and the trail builders designed the path to take advantage of that gift. God gives us water to quench our thirst and He gives us "spiritual water" through His promise of salvation given to mankind through the death and resurrection of His Son, Jesus Christ.

Water is essential to life. We have a responsibility as stewards of the trail to keep its water sources clean and sharable with other hikers. The "spiritual water" gifted to us through God's grace and mercy assures eternal life if only we accept it. And when we do accept it, we become followers of Christ. As builders and stewards of His trail, we are expected to chart our path so that it follows God's desired direction for us, to "fill our water bowls" from the studying of God's Word, and to share those resources with others.

Just as Hank found that the water in the stream was good and that it revived and sustained him on his hike, so can we be revived and sustained on our walk with Jesus by drinking daily from God's Word. We will certainly find that by charting our path according to God's will for us, the trail will provide. He will be there to make sure that our "water bowls" are full and that we always have fresh water to drink.

Related Bible Verses:

But whoever drinks the water I give them will never thirst. Indeed, the water I give them will become in them a spring of water welling up to eternal life. ~ John 4:14

Jesus said unto them, "I am the bread of life. Whoever comes to me will never go hungry, and whoever believes in me will never be thirsty. ~ John 6:35

Cheaha Falls

2

It's Cold and Dark

The day of hiking was long. The trek was hard, and in many places, quite difficult.

Hank did his usual excellent job of keeping to the trail and staying with his humans. In fact, most of the time, Hank stayed out front when he could be free to hike off the leash.

Hiking off the leash was something Hank looked forward to when the trail took the backpackers far enough into the back country that they were not very likely to encounter other hikers.

That particular day was very far back and deep into the wilderness. Hank had spent the entire day hiking in leash-less freedom. By the time the backpackers chose to end the day and select a site to make camp for the night, Hank was ready to stop and rest.

Camping in the backcountry of the Sipsey Wilderness Area in Alabama's Bankhead National Forest.

He was so eager to rest that he scarfed down his evening meal even faster than usual. He barely gave his human time to pitch the tent before he was sitting at the door wanting to get inside. Soon, Hank was stretched out in a sound sleep, all warm and cozy and dreaming about the day's adventure.

Hank wasn't afraid of or worried about the sounds filling the dark woods in the night. He wasn't worried about the night's chill preventing him from enjoying a restful sleep. Hank was well equipped by his human master to stay warm, and the sounds of the woodland creatures in the night were merely just musical lullabies.

As our Lord and Master, God takes care of us the same way. He wants us to feel safe and secure. He wants us to enjoy leash-less freedom from the daily struggles that can strap us down. He does not want us to worry or fear the things that "go bump in the night." He tells us this throughout the Bible.

Of course, there are many things that can keep us from having a good night's sleep. This just happens in a world that is filled with distractions that can easily overload our thoughts and fill our minds with anxiety so much that it can be almost impossible at times to fall asleep.

God understands this, but He tells us through Scripture that we should let go of those thoughts and trust Him to be in control. True, that can be extremely hard to do, but the more we study Scripture and the closer our relationship becomes with Him, the more we understand what God is telling us. It becomes easier to let Him guide our thoughts and actions.

Just as Hank knew his human master had prepared for his comfort and safety on the trail, we can know with all certainty that God, our Heavenly Master, has prepared for the comfort and safety of us as His children on our walk with Him.

Related Bible Verses:

When you lie down, you will not be afraid; when you lie down, your sleep will be sweet. ~ Proverbs 3:24

I lie down and sleep; I awake again, because the Lord sustains me. ~ Psalm 3:5

It's Cold and Dark ~ 5

Mount Cheaha Sunset

3
Keep Good Company

Flagg Mountain, near the small town of Weogufka, Alabama, is the southernmost official mountain in the Appalachian chain. It is only about an hour's drive from our home. Therefore, Hank has hiked there a number of times on the various loop trails throughout the area and along the well-known Pinhoti Trail, which has its southern terminus there.

Flagg Mountain is home to a small village of log cabins and a vintage fire tower that were built by the Civilian Conservation Corps (CCC) during the Great Depression of the 1930s. The history books tell us that the CCC was a major part of President Franklin D. Roosevelt's "New Deal" program. It provided badly needed jobs for young men during a time when the economy was at its lowest.

Hank and Sunny "Nimblewill Nomad" Eberhart: A more humble man would be hard to find.

The program also resulted in the construction of a number of facilities that are state parks today. The cabins, fire towers, and other structures built by those young men stand today as solidly as they did when first built. They display construction done with a sense of craftsmanship not seen in today's building techniques.

Flagg Mountain until recently was also home to one of the backpacking community's most famous and beloved individuals, Sunny "Nimblewill Nomad" Eberhart. Sunny served as the resident caretaker of the Flagg Mountain facilities. He holds the distinction of being the oldest individual to hike the full length of the

Keep Good Company ~ 7

Appalachian Trail (AT). At the age of eighty-three, he hiked from Flagg Mountain in Alabama to Mount Katahdin in Maine.

Hank made friends quickly with Sunny and visited him often. Theirs is a friendship that reminds one of the importance of choosing the company one keeps with care. Sunny is proud of his distinction as the oldest AT thru-hiker for sure, but he is as humble a man as one will ever meet.

Hank and I loved to hang out with Sunny, and Flagg Mountain is still one of our "happy places" for hiking and backpacking adventures.

God wants us to be aware of the company we keep. He wants us to surround ourselves with people of good character whose actions, speech, and treatment of others is upright and good. He also wants us to be humble. It is fine and wonderful to be proud of our accomplishments, and when those achievements are worthy, there really is no need for us to be boastful or to brag about them. They will be duly recognized and noted by others, and if we are following the path of God's will, they will become examples to help guide and influence others.

We should also remember that it is much easier to follow the path that the Lord desires for us when our friends and others in our life are not leading us astray. Moreover, others in our lives will lift us up and support us in our desire and efforts to follow the path God desires for us to walk.

Peer pressure is a real and sometimes difficult issue for young people, even for older people. We all need to be aware of the type of peer pressure that we allow ourselves to be influenced by. We also need to remember to be humble in our actions and behavior.

Related Bible Verses:

Do not be misled: Bad company corrupts good character. ~ 1 Corinthians 15:33

For those who exalt themselves will be humbled, and those who humble themselves will be exalted. ~ Matthew 23:12

Flagg Mountain Fire Tower

4

Leadership

Hank doesn't really care about history, but he does love to check things out as he encounters them along the trail. When the trail winds through an historic area and is marked by statues, that is even more intriguing.

The Pine Mountain Trail in Georgia's FDR State Park is one of those places. The hiking opportunities offered there are varied with some forty miles of multiple loop trails that all tie into the central spine of the twenty-three mile long Pine Mountain Trail.

FDR State Park is another among the wonderful legacies constructed through the CCC program. It is named in honor of President Franklin D. Roosevelt, who frequented that area of western Georgia. He also had a home in nearby Hot Springs, known today as "The Little White House," and is one of west Georgia's most visited tourist locations.

Hank "meets" President Franklin D. Roosevelt (FDR). This statue of FDR sits atop Dowdell Knob Overlook along Georgia's Pine Mountain Trail in the FDR State Park.

FDR also had a favorite spot on a high point that overlooks a part of the Pine Mountain Trail — Dowdell Knob — where he enjoyed picnicking and where he often came alone to find peace and solitude. Here is where he pondered the pressures and issues of being president of the United States during the troubling times of the Great Depression and as the nation was plunging into World War II.

Mr. Roosevelt was elected to three terms as president. This made him the only US president to serve more than two terms in office. As president, he tried to keep the United States neutral and out of the war. Following the bombing of the U.S. Naval base in Pearl Harbor, Hawaii by a surprise Japanese attack on December 7, 1941, remaining neutral was no longer an option.

This was before the days of TV or the Internet, so Americans learned of the attack over the radio. In his radio address to the American public, FDR is remembered for his words condemning the Pearl Harbor attack as "a date which will live in infamy." On December 11, Japan's allies, Nazi Germany, and Fascist Italy declared war on the United States. In response, the US formally joined the Allies and entered the European theater of war. (See Franklin D. Roosevelt, Wikipedia)

Mr. Roosevelt died in office in 1945 and did not live to see the end of World War II and the defeat of the Axis powers; however, he led our nation during a time of great turmoil and tremendous uncertainty. He is recognized by historians as one of the greatest presidents in American history.

God tells us in Scripture what is required of a good leader. He tells us that a good leader must not be arrogant, quick-tempered, a drunkard, violent, or greedy for gain. A good leader is hospitable, a lover of good, self-controlled, upright, holy, and disciplined.

There are many personalities described in the Bible as being good leaders, such as David, Moses, the wise King Solomon, and others. Jesus Himself, the greatest and most perfect among all leaders, followed a fixed set of principles and truths — God's Word. He led by example as He showed concern and love toward others. He was selfless and put His own needs second to the needs of others. He ministered to others and taught that good leaders are accountable not only for their own actions, but also for their very thoughts.

As followers of Christ, we all share leadership qualities and potential and have opportunities to use and develop them. We are even expected to do so. Scripture can guide us as we develop and use those skills.

We are not and will never be perfect as Jesus was, but unless those who see our actions can see us striving and improving, they will not be able to look to us for example, and they will see us as less than fully serious about the things to be done.

Few of us will ever have to step into the kind of position of leadership that challenged President Roosevelt, but we all will have opportunities to be leaders and to influence others many times in small ways, but sometimes, in large ones. We should read and study God's guide for how to lead. A good leader should study Scripture.

Related Bible Verses:

Not so with you. Instead, whoever wants to become great among you must be your servant. ~ Matthew 20:26

If a king judges the poor with fairness, his throne will be established forever. ~ Proverbs 29:14

5

Trust Him

The Grayson Highlands of Virginia offer some of the most spectacular and most breathtaking scenery found along the Appalachian Trail.

The focal point of the Grayson Highlands State Park is located in Grayson County, Virginia. The area adjoins the Mount Rogers National Recreation Area and lies within the Jefferson National Forest.

Grayson Highlands State Park comprises some 4,502 acres, but the highlands covers much more area along the trail. The highlands is also home to some famously known herds of wild ponies who roam and graze freely there.

Hank meets one of the wild ponies in the Grayson Highlands.

The ponies were introduced to the Grayson Highlands in the 1970s; however, they are semi-confined by fencing that surrounds the Grayson Highlands State Park as well as fencing within the national forest sections. They help to maintain the mountain balds (the areas without many trees) by eating grass and small shrubs. (Ponies of the Grayson Highlands "Appalachian Voice" app voices.org)

There are some ten to fifteen herds of these wild ponies throughout the Grayson Highlands, and over the years, they have become accustomed to human presence. It is relatively easy to walk very close to some of the ponies. In fact, some will even let one pet them, but it is strongly urged by park officials that humans do not feed the ponies because some will bite.

The ponies of Grayson Highlands and the Mount Rogers National Recreation Area not only provide a necessary resource to maintain the open mountain balds, but also draw tourism to the park.

Hank found the wild ponies to be a curiosity. He had never seen one before hiking through the area. They looked like strange big dogs, and since Hank almost never has trouble making new friends, why not introduce himself to one?

Both Hank and the pony were timid at first. Being unsure and because it is a rule to have pets on a leash in the state park area, Hank's human cautiously and carefully let him approach the equally curious pony.

As things turned out, there was no reason for much concern. The two animals touched noses in the way that animals seem to greet one another in an introductory encounter. They visited for a few moments, then Hank went on his hiking way while the curious pony rejoined its herd and continued leisurely grazing the grass along the trail.

Hank's human had trust concerns about letting Hank get too close to the wild pony, but neither Hank nor the pony showed any such caution. They were simply wanting to meet and experience the new contact.

Trust issues are a fixture in today's world. So many fears challenge our natural curiosity to explore and experience new things. God does not want us to be reckless with our trust. Moreover, He set guidelines and instructions, and advises us throughout Scripture about how to use that trust in ways that will not only protect us, but will also bring Him glory and honor.

This starts with our trust in God. God tells us to trust in Him with all of our heart and lean not on our own understanding (Proverbs 3:5). This means that God expects us to trust in Him no matter what happens. We need to believe every word He tells us, and know that whatever He has promised us will come to pass no matter how long it takes.

Trust is akin to faith, and faith and trust in God can be developed by spending time in God's Word, learning to trust Him even in small things, and through listening to others' testimonies. As you do this, your faith and trust in God will deepen.

We will begin to learn that God expects us to share our own testimonies with others as we grow. Our testimony is simply our personal story about how God has blessed and enriched our own lives. Think about it, if something good and wonderful happens to you, you naturally want to share that news with others. What could be more wonderful than receiving one's salvation?

As we grow in our faith and trust in God, we grow in our relationship with Him. Mutual trust is the foundation for close relationships. Trust is the ability to believe in the good intentions and good will of another toward us in a relationship. Learning to trust another is among our earliest life lessons.

So, when we are presented with a new opportunity to meet others and share the promise and blessings that God offers, we should remember to let go of nervous fears. Trust in God to help you find a way to share that story, and trust that the opportunity to share it will be met with good intentions.

Related Bible Verses:

But the fruit of the Spirit is love, joy, peace, forbearance, kindness, goodness, faithfulness. ~ Galatians 5:22

Trust in the Lord with all your heart, and do not lean on your own understanding. In all your ways acknowledge him, and he will make your paths straight. ~ Proverbs 3:5-6

Wild Pony Herd - Grayson Highlands, Virginia

6

Follow the Blaze

Hiking trails are typically marked with colored "blazes" of paint on trees, rocks, posts, or some other reasonably permanent fixture to show the way.

Every trail has a blaze color that is specific to that trail. That way, hikers know that as long as they follow the blaze associated with that particular trail, they are on the right path.

Hank follows the white-blazed trail through the rocky pathway on the Appalachian Trail.

In most situations, trail blazes are pretty easily visible and recognizable; however, there are times when the blaze may be faded and difficult to see. The blaze may have been painted on a tree that was blown down in a storm, or, on a rock or boulder that has since been covered with leaf litter or other ground debris, making it virtually non-existent.

Hank is always a good, smart dog on the trail. He has a sense about him (probably his extremely keen sense of smell) that always enables him to know exactly where the path is. He has become so accustomed to trail hiking that he often hikes ahead of his human pals, but he never lets them out of his sight. If they lag behind, Hank stops and waits for them to catch up. If the trail forks, he stops and waits until his humans determine which fork to take. Many times, he has enabled his human hiking pals to prevent becoming lost, because he could find the trail when they couldn't.

Follow the Blaze ~ 17

Hank does not read trail blazes, but he always knows. He trusts his detection senses. He has been right so many times when his human pals were wrong, that the declaration, "Trust Hank, he is on it," has become the consensus of agreement when trail blazes are not to be found.

That is the way it is with God. He uses His Word to serve as our blaze to show us the way.

The Bible refers to this as "lighting the way." Light in the Bible is a symbol of learning, illumination, and intelligence. When we "follow the light," we are following the direction God has set for our lives.

We receive God's light through a variety of ways. Those include praying and seeking God's will by asking, participating in the life and worship of the church, reading and reflecting on the Scriptures, and opening our lives to the Holy Spirit.

We need to always be following the blaze God provides to show us the way. In those times and situations when something has obscured the blaze and determining what to do and which way to go becomes a difficult challenge, remember Hank. Trust your senses. Trust in the Lord. Remember that His blaze is the truth and the light. If we follow God's blaze, we will never become lost. For we are saved and we are assured to be following the right path.

Related Bible Verses:

The Lord makes firm the steps of the one who delights in him. Though he may stumble, he will not fall, for the Lord upholds him with his hand. ~ Psalm 37:23-24

Your word is a lamp for my feet, a light on my path. ~ Psalm 119:105

7
Carry Your Weight

Backpacking means carrying everything that one needs to live on the trail for an extended period of time.

We naturally conjure up the image of the hiker bent over under the weight of a heavy backpack. And rightfully so, because that backpack contains the hiker's food, shelter, clothing, bedding, water, and other essentials needed for sustaining their survival on the trip.

Hank is a strong dog, but he has to eat a bit more on the trail than he does at home to replace the calories

Hank carries his own food for his journeys, but his load is light enough for him to easily manage it.

that he burns hiking for many miles each day. So, he has his own backpack, and, carries his own food.

Hank carries a shared load, but his human doesn't weigh him down with more of a burden than he can easily and safely carry. In fact, veterinarians say that a dog can carry up to 10 percent of their body weight. At that rate, being a ninety pound dog, Hank could safely carry up to nine pounds in his pack, but his human has him carry only the amount of food needed for the trip, which has never exceeded five pounds. His human carries Hank's bedding, cold weather gear, water, and other essentials.

That is the way God treats us as His children. He shares our burdens and helps us to manage them in times when they may become heavy.

The burdens that we carry are not all weight-bearing, such as with a loaded backpack. They sometimes are emotional burdens. Sometimes they are responsibilities for work, family, school, or even responsibilities that we face in our actions and relationships with friends and others in our lives. Sometimes, they are even the burdens being borne by our friends and others who we know.

As God's children, we are held accountable for our actions. Our actions are expected to be good and right and such that they serve others and bring Him glory and honor. We are called to serve others. That is, we are supposed to help others carry their burdens whenever that is possible. This does not mean only physical burdens, but also to show empathy or sympathy in situations where someone might be suffering sadness, grief, or pain.

When we need help ourselves, God is also there for us. He tells us to cast our burdens upon Him. That means that He wants to help us with our problems and concerns no matter how small or how large. Even though sometimes we might think that God is not listening, He is. He will answer our pleas for help in His way and in His time. God knows what we need far better than we know ourselves. He just asks us to trust Him.

When you pour your heart out to God in prayer and set your eyes on Him, you gain perspective. You have direct access to God. Trust Him with everything in your life — your relationships, finances, pain, job, school, passions, hopes, disappointments, failures, and wins. He cares for you. When you trust God with everything, He will defend you, help you, and sustain you. He will help you to bear your burdens.

Related Bible Verses:

Carry each other's burdens, and in this way you will fulfill the law of Christ. ~ Galatians 6:2

Cast your cares on the Lord and he will sustain you; he will never let the righteous be shaken. ~ Psalm 55:22

Sunset Along the Trail - Grayson Highlands

8

Feed the Spirit

Eating on the trail is no small deal. Actually, it's a pretty big deal.

Hikers and backpackers need in the range of 3,000 calories per day. This translates in weight to about 1.5 pounds of food per day.

Exactly how much an individual hiker needs depends on his or her metabolism, but 1.5 pounds of food - or 3,000 calories - is a good place to start.

Hank is good sized dog. At ninety pounds, he needs about 1,225 calories in his normal daily diet. On average, the extra calories needed for a dog engaging in an endurance-type activity, such as hiking, is about .8 calories per pound of its body weight per mile traveled. If I calculate this correctly, at ninety pounds of body weight hiking over eight to ten miles a day, Hank needs between 576 and 720 calories over the amount of his routine daily diet. Because of that, Hank should eat a little more while on the trail.

Midday feeding time on the trail. Hank gets a full ration feeding each morning. He gets a half ration feeding at midday.

He does and doesn't mind the extra food at all. Hank is a true "chow hound" when it comes to food. He never refuses it. In fact, he would eat his food and then eat yours, too, if you let him.

Hank is well fed, but he always is anxious for more.

God gives us the Bible as our source of daily spiritual food and to also be our source during times when our daily diet needs to be supplemented such as during times of difficulty, times of great emotional stress, or when we are wrestling with difficult decisions and the pressures that life can put on us. Those are the times when "extra trail miles" require "extra calories." Studying the Bible provides us with an energy that fills us on a multi-dimensional level. That includes physical, mental, emotional, and spiritual needs.

Even in normal times we all need a routine daily diet of God's Word; however, we sometimes find ourselves facing times of great endurance. Not unlike Hank and his hiking friends, those times require an even larger feeding.

When we immerse ourselves in the study of Scripture, we should be like Hank — always anxious for more. It is through the study of God's Word in the Scriptures that we feed our spirit. This is how we open our hearts to receive God's teachings. The more we read and study His Scripture, the more we learn, grow spiritually, and grow a closer relationship with God.

Related Bible Verses:

I am the living bread that came down from heaven, Whoever eats this bread will live forever. This bread is my flesh, which I will give for the life of the world. ~ John 6:51

Like new-born babies, crave pure spiritual milk, so that by it you may grow up in your salvation, ~ 1 Peter 2:2

Dawn Along the Roan Highlands of the Appalachian Trail

9
Rest is Best

Hank can hike for a long time. He maintains a steady speed and doesn't walk too fast or too slow. More importantly, he knows when to pause for a rest.

Every year, hundreds of hikers set out to complete the thousands of miles that make up the country's long distance trails, such as the Appalachian Trail, the Pacific Crest Trail, and the Continental Divide Trail among others.

Every year, the majority of those hikers drop out and don't complete the journey.

Hank pauses to rest as he ascends up the mountain trail.

Reasons for leaving the trail before reaching their goal are numerous. A hiker's decision to stop is an individual one. More often than not, though, most give up because they gave out.

Trekking hundreds or thousands of miles in wild backcountry terrain takes a tremendous toll on one's body. Physical exhaustion sets in quickly, followed at some point by mental and emotional exhaustion. To complete the arduous journey involved with hiking a backcountry trail for days, weeks, and months on end requires discipline and rest.

Outpacing his human hiking pals is easy for Hank. He could stay yards out front without expending a great deal of effort, yet he paces his speed. When he gets a significant degree of distance between him and his humans, he simply sits down and rests while his humans plod along to eventually catch up to him.

Rest is Best ~ 25

Hank has learned the importance of rest to enable him to endure long days along the trail.

God tells us that rest is key to enabling us to endure and complete the journey that He desires for us as His followers.

God Himself even took a day of rest after He created the world. After taking six days to create the world, God took the seventh day as a day of rest (Genesis 2:1-3). He directs us to do likewise.

The Bible talks a great deal about the importance of rest. God tells us that we need not only physical rest, but mental and spiritual rest, as well. Spiritual rest is akin to trust and faith. As God's followers, we are instructed to "rest in the Lord." What that means is that we are to be still; to listen to what God is telling us through His Word and as we pray. When we rest in the Lord, we begin to hear and understand Him more clearly.

Related Bible Verses:

Truly my soul finds rest in God; my salvation comes from him. ~ Psalm 62:1

Come to me, all you who are weary and burdened, and I will give you rest. ~ Matthew 11:28

Hank takes a rest on a cool trail rock.

A Restful Scene Along the Trail

10

Joy is Strength

Hank looks forward to the end of a long day of hiking. He loves the hike, but he also loves to chill once the walking is done.

He has a favorite game at the end of the day that his human pals call "rock soccer." Hank finds a rock and begins to roll it about with his nose and shuffle it with his paws — just like a soccer player does with the ball. Hank has tried a ball, but he prefers a rock.

He can play this game almost nonstop for a long time before finally giving it up for bedtime (which he also enjoys). It's funny to watch him play and it's pretty entertaining. It is also amazing that after walking for many miles, Hank still has the strength and energy to play with so much enthusiasm.

Pack off and it's time to play.

It is quite evident that Hank receives a great deal of joy out of his game of rock soccer.

The title of this story comes from words spoken by Mother Teresa. Mother Teresa was a Catholic nun who spent her life in the slums of India caring for the sick, dying, and destitute. She said, "Joy is prayer. Joy is strength. Joy is love. Joy is a net of love by which you can catch souls." (brainy quote.com)

God wants us to find joy and happiness in our lives. He wants us to let that joy flow from us in all that we do and in our service to others. When we share our joy, we bring honor to God.

Having joy includes feeling happy and cheerful, but that is not all of it. The ability to feel and show joy comes from God Himself. It is not rooted in the source of favorable circumstances, but from the strength that we have as followers of Christ. Joy in the Lord is something that we cannot lose. It is a spiritual quality that lasts forever. We always have it.

The Bible says, "The joy of the Lord is my strength" (Nehemiah 8:10). The joy that is found in God's presence isn't static; it transforms and regenerates us.

He gives us strength to follow Him along the path where He guides us.

The Bible says many times that God gives us joy and peace. If we follow His teachings through studying Scripture, just like Hank finds the strength to play and enjoy his game of rock soccer at the end of the day, we will find our strength and joy overflowing.

Related Bible Verses:

... I have told you this so that my joy may be in you and that your joy may be complete. ~ John 15:10-11

The Lord has done it this very day; let us rejoice today and be glad. ~ Psalm 118:24

But the fruit of the Spirit is love, joy, peace, forbearance, kindness, goodness, faithfulness, gentleness and self-control. ~ Galatians 5:22-23

The Joy of God's Creation - Roan Highlands

11

Peace, Be Still

There is a hiking trail in Italy known as the Walk of Peace.

The Walk of Peace trail connects the Alps to the Adriatic Sea and follows along the former World War I frontline that once straddled the mountainous border between Italy and the present-day Republic of Slovenia (formerly a part of Yugoslavia).

For some 137 miles, the Walk of Peace passes through picturesque villages, over cathedral-like mountain peaks, past tranquil glacial lakes, across gentle flowing rivers, and perhaps most importantly, it serves as a living history lesson.

Taking time to enjoy the gifts of the trail.

Hank has never hiked the Walk of Peace trail in Europe. He likely may never do so, but he has hiked over hundreds of miles of trails that each in its own right has served as a walk of peace.

Many hikers talk about finding an inner peace and calm as they walk along the trail surrounded by the beauty of God's creation. A quick and easy Google search produces numerous quotes touting the peace and calm found through hiking:

"An early morning walk is a blessing for the whole day." – Henry David Thoreau

"Go out I beg of you and taste the beauty of the wild. Behold the miracle of the earth with all the wonder of a child." – Edna Jaques

"Of all the paths you take in life, make sure a few of them are dirt." – John Muir

"Not all those who wander are lost." – J.R.R. Tolkien

... And there are many more. (see wonder-lush.org)

In the Book of Mark, Jesus uttered the words "Peace, be still" (Mark 4:39 KJV). He said this to calm a great storm that arose as Jesus and His disciples crossed over the Sea of Galilee in a small boat. This can also be found in the books of Matthew, Luke, and John, and various translations use different wordings that still tell us the same thing.

Peace, be still is God telling us that He is in control. He will calm the storms that we face in our lives. He will see us through times of trouble and difficulties. He will give us inner peace and calm, but we have to trust Him!

Peace given to us by God is a peace of the heart and mind. This does not mean that as Christians we no longer have to face difficulty and stressful situations. We do, but it does mean that if we entrust those situations to God, He will help us navigate our way through them. He will grant us inner peace and calm in those times.

God sent His Son, Jesus, to be the bridge between God and mankind. And it is by acknowledging and accepting Jesus as our Savior that we receive that peace.

When we live in God's grace and goodness and are following His will for us, we experience this peace.

Recall the J.R.R. Tolkien quote cited earlier in this story? Unfortunately, some are lost, but God's grace and mercy provide a way by which anyone who accepts His gift of salvation will be found and saved. As His children, we are charged to search out those who are still lost and to help bring them back to God through Jesus.

God wants everyone to receive His gift of peace.

Related Bible Verses:

I have told you these things, so that in me you may have peace. In this world you will have trouble. But take heart! I have overcome the world. ~ John 16:33

Do not be anxious about anything, but in every situation, by prayer and petition, with thanksgiving, present your requests to God. And the peace of God, which transcends all understanding, will guard your hearts and minds in Christ Jesus. ~ Philippians 4:6-7

Whatever you have learned or received or heard from me, or seen in me—put it into practice. And the God of peace will be with you. ~ Philippians 4:9

Peace, Be Still

12

Finish Well

Hank's home state of Alabama offers a set of trails that are recognized as "The Alabama Triple Crown of Backpacking" (ATC).

The ATC is sixty miles total and is comprised of three twenty-mile loop sections. The first is the Chin-Pin-Skyway loop in the Cheaha Wilderness/Cheaha State Park area in Northeast-Central Alabama, named for the three trails included in this loop — the Chinabee Silent Trail, Pinhoti Trail, and the Skyway Trail. The second is a twenty-mile loop in the Oak Mountain State Park near Birmingham that includes a hike out to the famous King's Chair Overlook. And the third is a twenty-mile loop through the Sipsey Wilderness Area of the Bankhead National Forest of Northwest Alabama.

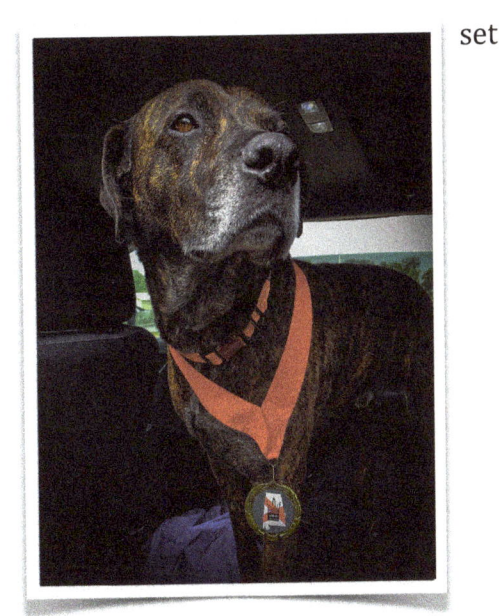

Hank with his ATC hiking medal

The ATC is intended to be hiked over three consecutive days with each loop being a twenty-mile day hike.

Hank hikes with his human pals who are older, slower, and not really interested in completing these long trails as rapidly as they are intended to be hiked. Hank and his humans did complete the three ATC loops — even though they hiked them as extended, overnight, trips — and earlier in 2022, Hank was recognized as being the first canine on record to complete the designated ATC hikes in total. Because of that, he was awarded an ATC completion medal by the program organizer.

As the photograph accompanying this story shows, Hank looks to be very regal and proud wearing his ATC hiking medal. He likes it for sure. It is a positive reinforcement, and Hank basks in positive reinforcement.

We all like to win, and God wants us to win. That is why the Bible is not only filled with good news about salvation, but is also our positive reinforcement. It tells us that every one of us who is part of God's team is a winner. As part of God's team, we have won victory over sin. Our reward is eternal life at the winner's podium beside Christ.

The Bible also tells us how to walk in our victory: "... if we walk in the light, as he is in the light, we have fellowship one with another, and the blood of Jesus, his Son, purifies us from all sin" (1 John 1:7-10).

So, how do we know that we are walking in victory?

We walk in victory when we are obedient to God, when we remove the impurity of sin, when we pray and meditate on God's Word, when we focus on God, when we persevere through our trials, when we persevere in our faith, and when we submit to God.

How do we live a life of victory?

We are conscious of our thoughts. We strive to keep our thoughts clean and focused on the teachings that God tells us in the Bible. We love and serve others and surround ourselves with things and with people that reflect the kind of life that we want to live as God's children. And we never give up.

It is not an always easy path to follow. Very often, in fact, it is very difficult to stay the course in the world that we live in, but God gives us His Word to guide us and instruct us. Through a consistent study of Scripture, we gain not only hope, guidance, and encouragement, but we also gain wisdom, understanding, courage, knowledge, compassion, and growth as we walk daily in our relationship with our Lord.

May we so live to enjoy that day when the Lord may say to us, "Well done, good and faithful servant" (Matthew 25:21).

Related Bible Verses:

... anyone who competes as an athlete does not receive the victor's crown, except by competing according to the rules. ~ 2 Timothy 2:5

Do you not know that in a race all the runners run, but only one gets the prize? Run in such a way as to get the prize. ~ 1 Corinthians 9:24-25

For everyone born of God overcomes the world. This is the victory that has overcome the world, even our faith. ~ 1 John 5:4

Hank the Hiking Hound - A World Class and Faithful Dog

A Backpacker's Prayer

Lord, show me the path of Your will for my life.

Make Your blaze visible so that I do not lose my way.

Help me to bear up under my load and to always remember that
You are there in times when my load becomes heavy and difficult.

Feed my hunger with Your bread of life,
and quench my thirst from the flowing spring of Your Holy Spirit.

For You are the Creator of all that is good and beautiful
and Master over everything.

Help me to do good unto others and in the sight of others,
so that I may be an acceptable steward of Your trail,
and so that I may help show others the way as You have instructed.

Give me wisdom to plan well.

Make me humble in my needs.

Grant me courage to complete the tasks at hand.

Let me always be thankful for Your blessings
and to always remember that through Your grace and mercy,
the trail will provide.

Amen.

Mitch Emmons
2022